Hal Leonard Student Piano Library

Piano Solos

Book 1

FOREWORD

Piano Solos presents challenging original music that coordinates page-by-page with the **Piano Lessons** and **Piano Practice Games** books in the **Hal Leonard Student Piano Library**. The outstanding variety of composers and musical styles makes every solo an important piece in its own right – exciting to both performer and listener. In addition, each piece is designed to encourage and ensure further mastery of the concepts and skills in the **Piano Lessons** books.

May these **Piano Solos** become favorite pieces that delight all who hear and play them.

Best wishes,

ISBN 978-0-7935-6262-6

HAL•LEONARD®

Visit Hal Leonard Online at
www.halleonard.com

World headquarters, contact:
Hal Leonard
7777 West Bluemound Road
Milwaukee, WI 53213
Email: info@halleonard.com

In Europe, contact:
Hal Leonard Europe Limited
1 Red Place
London, W1K 6PL
Email: info@halleonardeurope.com

In Australia, contact:
Hal Leonard Australia Pty. Ltd.
4 Lentara Court
Cheltenham, Victoria, 3192 Australia
Email: info@halleonard.com.au

Authors
Barbara Kreader, Fred Kern, Phillip Keveren, Mona Rejino

Consultants
Tony Caramia, Bruce Berr, Richard Rejino

Editor
Anne Wester

Illustrator
Fred Bell

CONTENTS

*✔

* *Students can check pieces as they play them.*

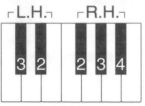

Water Lily

Delicately

Phillip Keveren

With accompaniment, student starts here:

Delicately (♩ = 95)

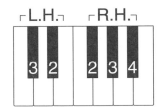

Mister Machine

Bill Boyd

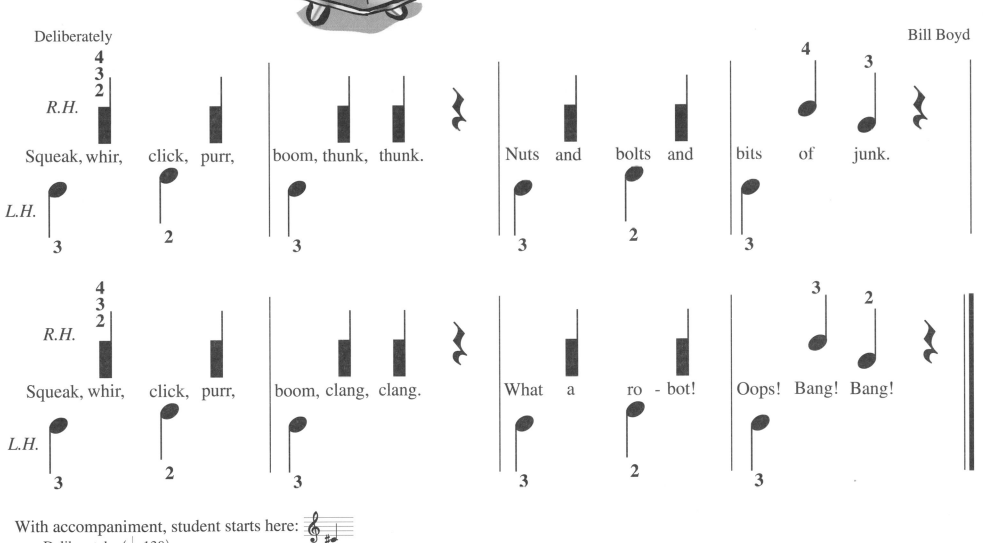

Use with Lesson Book 1, pg. 18

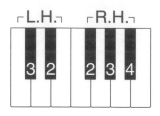

Walking The Dog

Lazy

Fred Kern

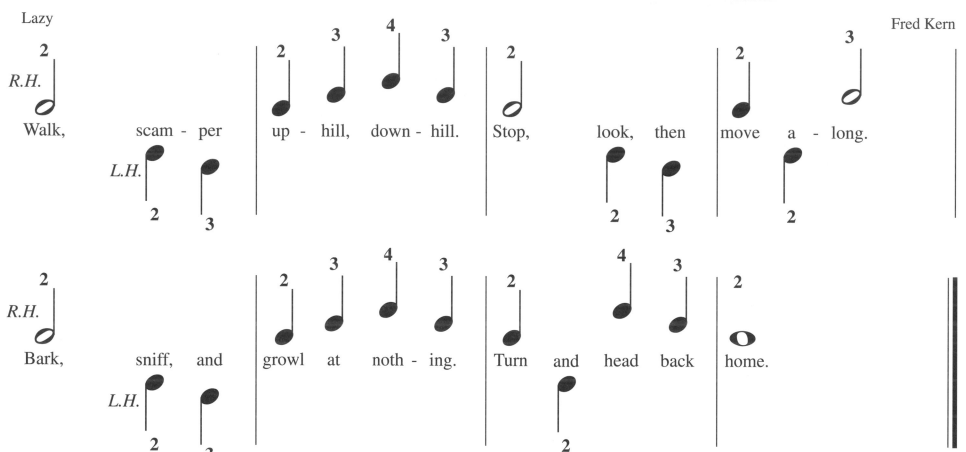

R.H.

Walk, scam - per | up - hill, down - hill. | Stop, look, then | move a - long.

L.H.

R.H.

Bark, sniff, and | growl at noth - ing. | Turn and head back | home.

L.H.

With accompaniment, student starts here:

Lazy ($\sqrt{3}$) ($\quarternote = 105$)

mp

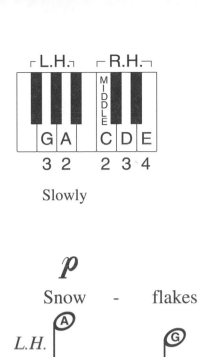

Quiet Night

Bill Boyd

Slowly

p

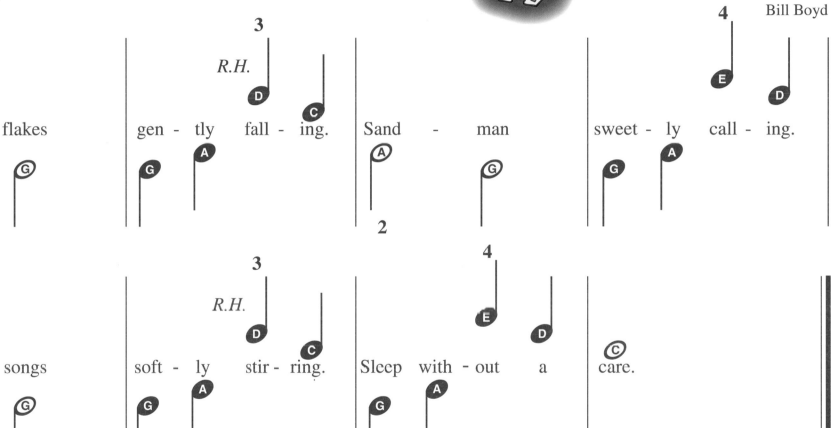

Snow - flakes gen - tly fall - ing. Sand - man sweet - ly call - ing.

Wind songs soft - ly stir - ring. Sleep with - out a care.

With accompaniment, student starts here:

Slowly (♩=88)

p

With pedal

Use with Lesson Book 1, pg. 31

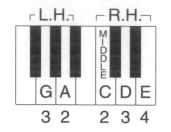

Bear Dance

Somewhat heavily

Christos Tsitsaros

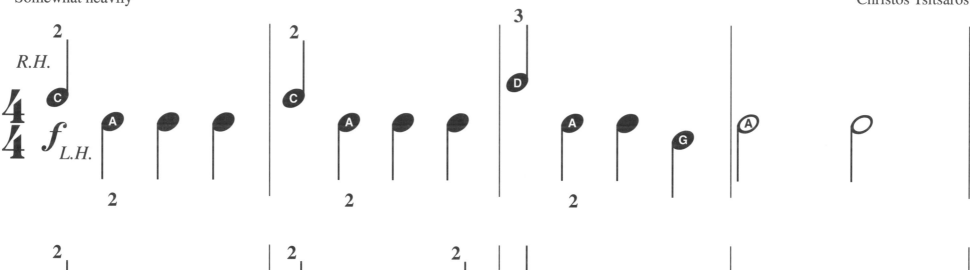

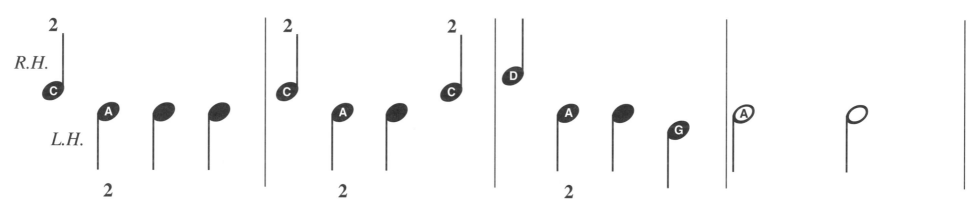

With accompaniment, student starts here:

Somewhat heavily (♩ = 150)

Stomp Dance

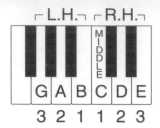

Carol Klose

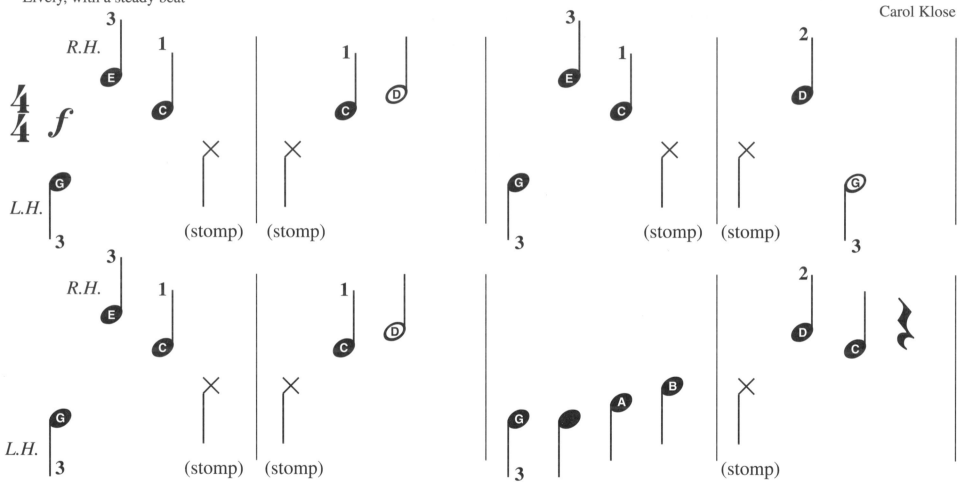

With accompaniment, student starts here:

Lively, with a steady beat

Use with Lesson Book 1, pg. 33

8

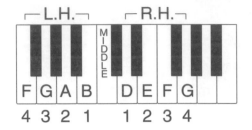

Howard H. Hippo

Heavily plodding

Phillip Keveren

f Did you know my hip - po's kind of slow? But when he

For solo performance, this piece may be played one octave lower than written.

Accompaniment (Student plays one octave higher than written.)

Heavily plodding (♩ = 115)

mf

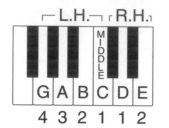

Wishful Thinking

Mona Rejino

Smoothly

Some day, some - where, I will make my wish come true.

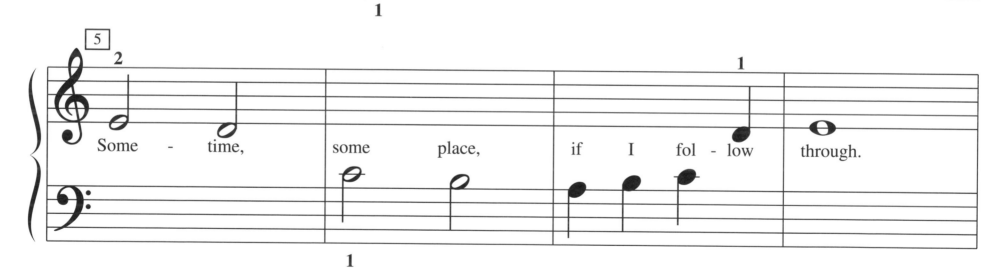

Some - time, some place, if I fol - low through.

Accompaniment (Student plays one octave higher than written.)

Smoothly (♩ = 105)

With pedal

Use with Lesson Book 1, pg. 43

12

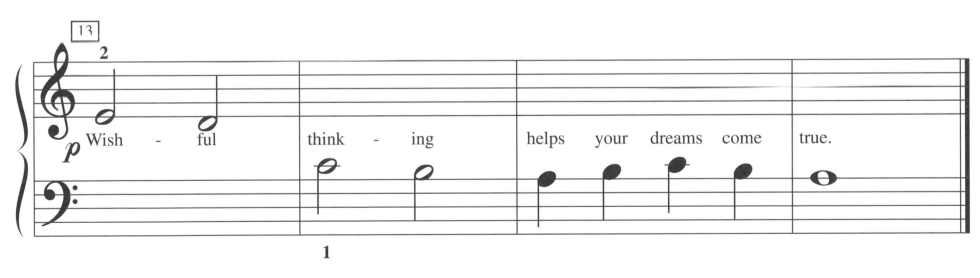

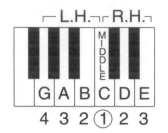

Toes In The Sand

This song can be expanded by improvising on A B C D E as shown on the next page!

Phillip Keveren

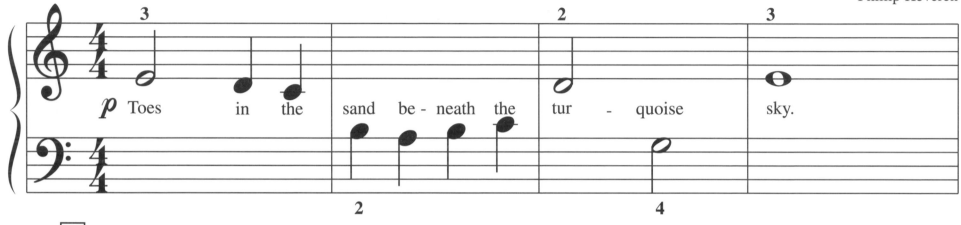

Toes in the sand be-neath the tur - quoise sky.

Build - ing a cas - tle, gen - tle waves wash by.

Accompaniment (Student plays one octave higher than written.)

Continue to next page for improvisation.

Use with Lesson Book 1, pg. 44

Keep your hands in the A B C D E position.

Listen and feel the pulse as your teacher plays the accompaniment below. When you are ready, make up your own song by mixing the notes in any order you want.

Play the eight-measure melody on page 14, improvise a bit on page 15, then return to the main melody (the "head" in jazz slang) at the beginning of the piece.

Repeat ad lib.

Student returns to head.

15

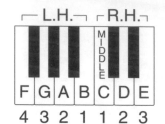

Whistling Tune

Leisurely

Fred Kern

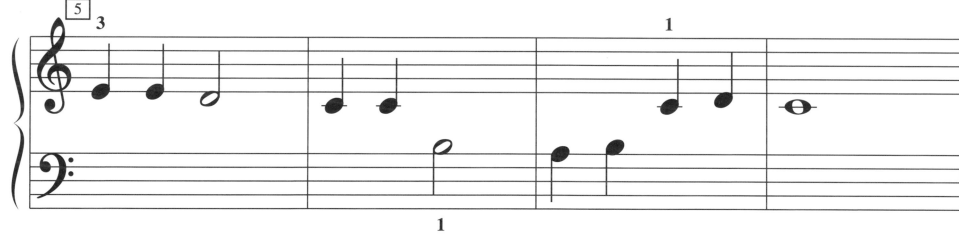

Accompaniment (Student plays one octave higher than written.)

Leisurely (♩ = 120)

Use with Lesson Book 1, pg. 46

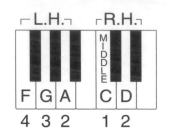

Struttin'

Mona Rejino

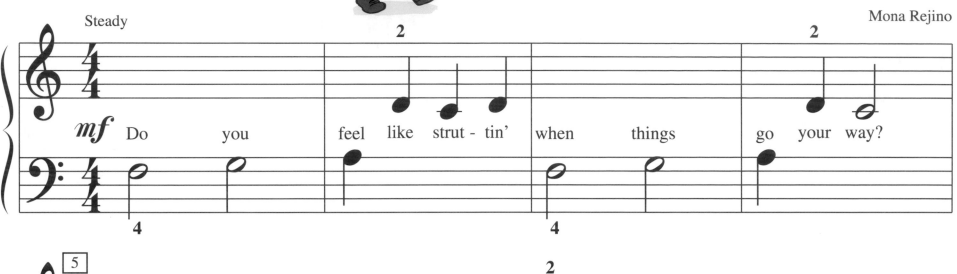

Steady

mf Do you feel like strut - tin' when things go your way?

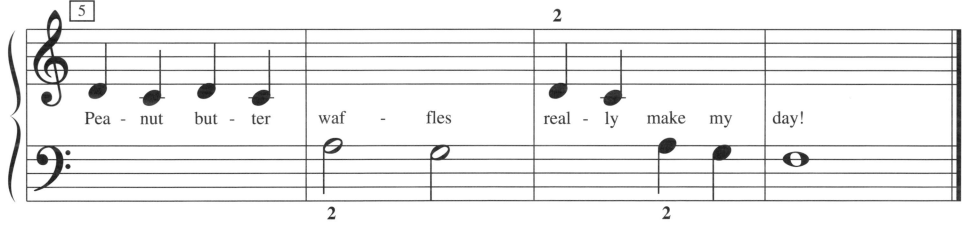

5 Pea - nut but - ter waf - fles real - ly make my day!

Accompaniment (Student plays one octave higher than written.)

Steady (♩ = 135)

mp

Old Saw*

Fred Kern

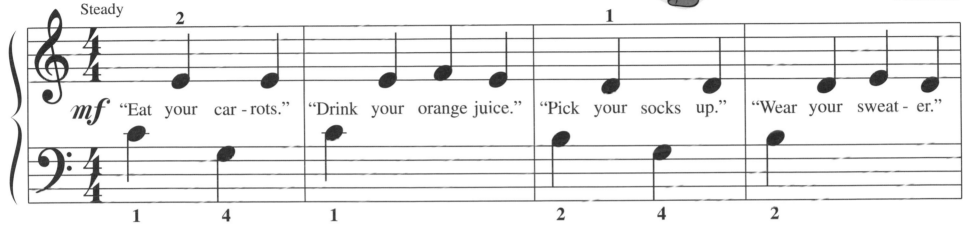

Steady

mf "Eat your car-rots." "Drink your orange juice." "Pick your socks up." "Wear your sweat-er."

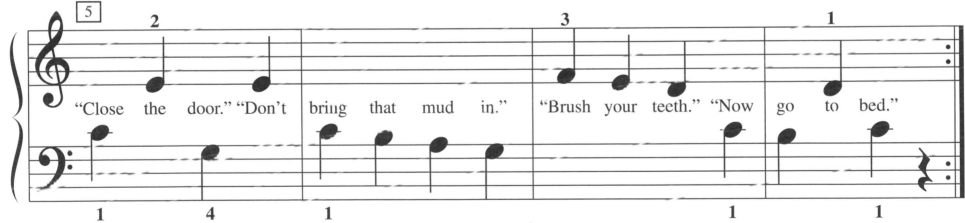

[5] "Close the door." "Don't bring that mud in." "Brush your teeth." "Now go to bed."

An old "saw" is a saying used so often that it becomes commonplace.

Accompaniment (Student plays one octave higher than written.)

Steady (♩ - 130)

mp

Use with Lesson Book 1, pg. 48

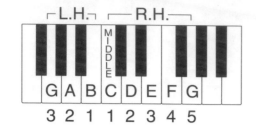

By The River's Edge

Quietly flowing along

Carol Klose

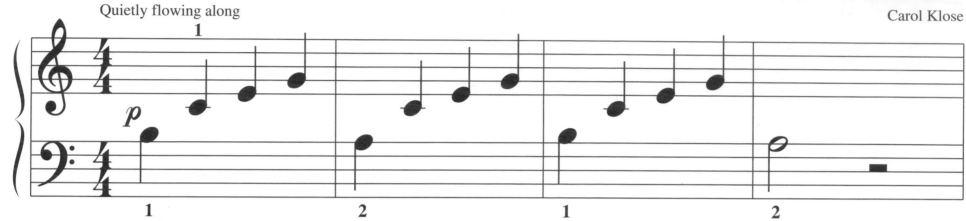

For solo performance, this piece may be played one octave higher than written with damper pedal held down throughout.

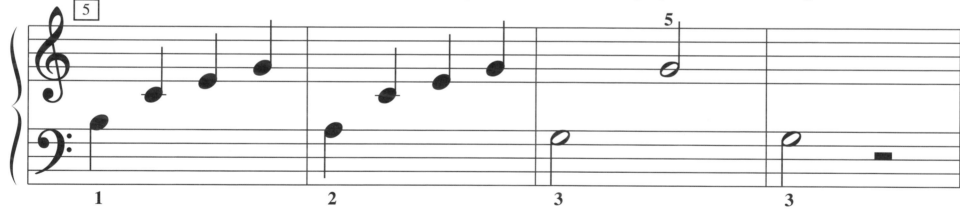

Accompaniment (Student plays two octaves higher than written.)

Quietly flowing along (♩ = 120)

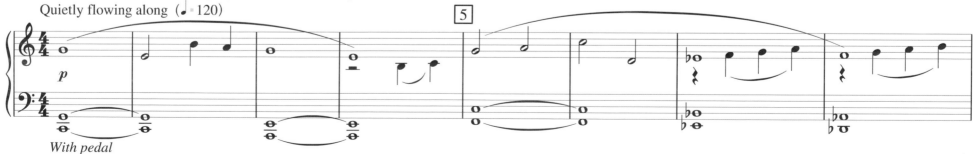

With pedal

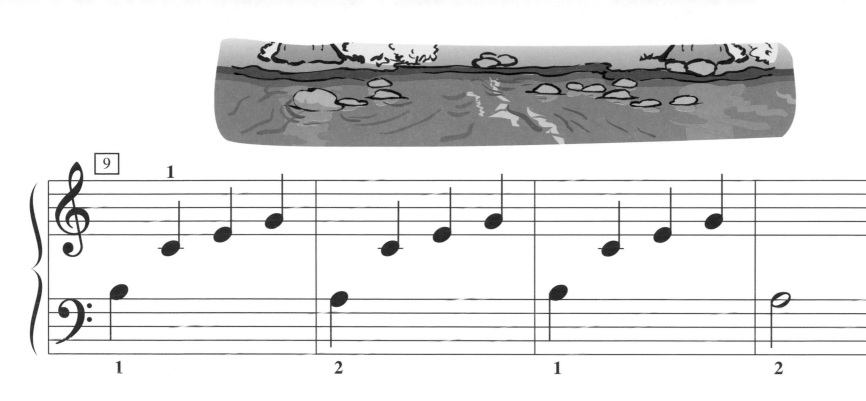

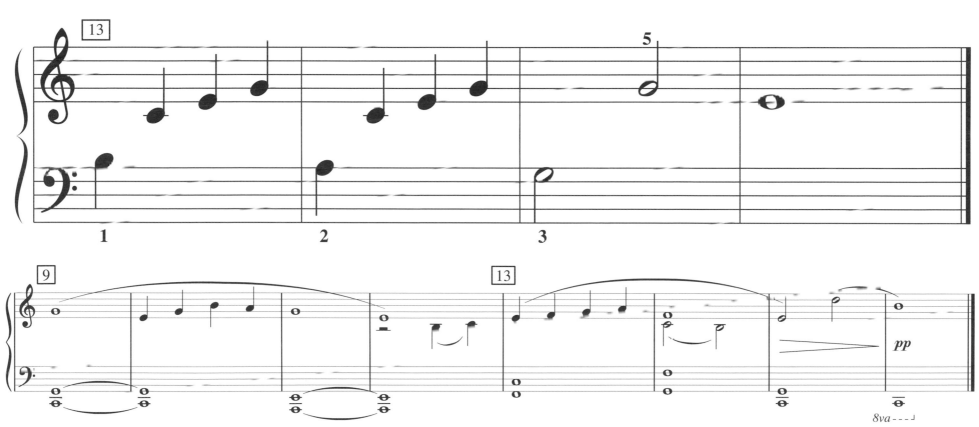

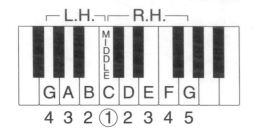

The Wild Rest

Bill Boyd

Moderately

mf Rest, wild rest, you do your best to trick me.

Rest, you pest, you test my skill. I

Accompaniment (Student plays one octave higher than written.)

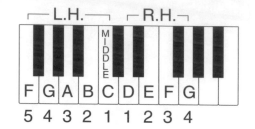

Moving Away

Italo Taranta

Slowly

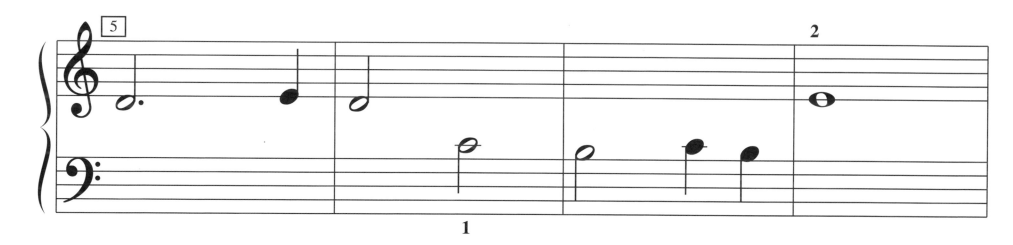

Accompaniment (Student plays one octave higher than written.)

Slowly ($\quad$ = 120)

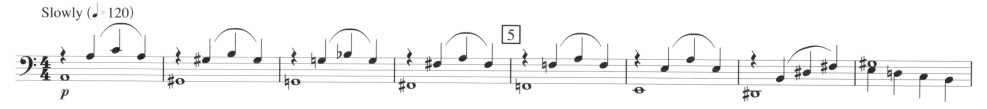

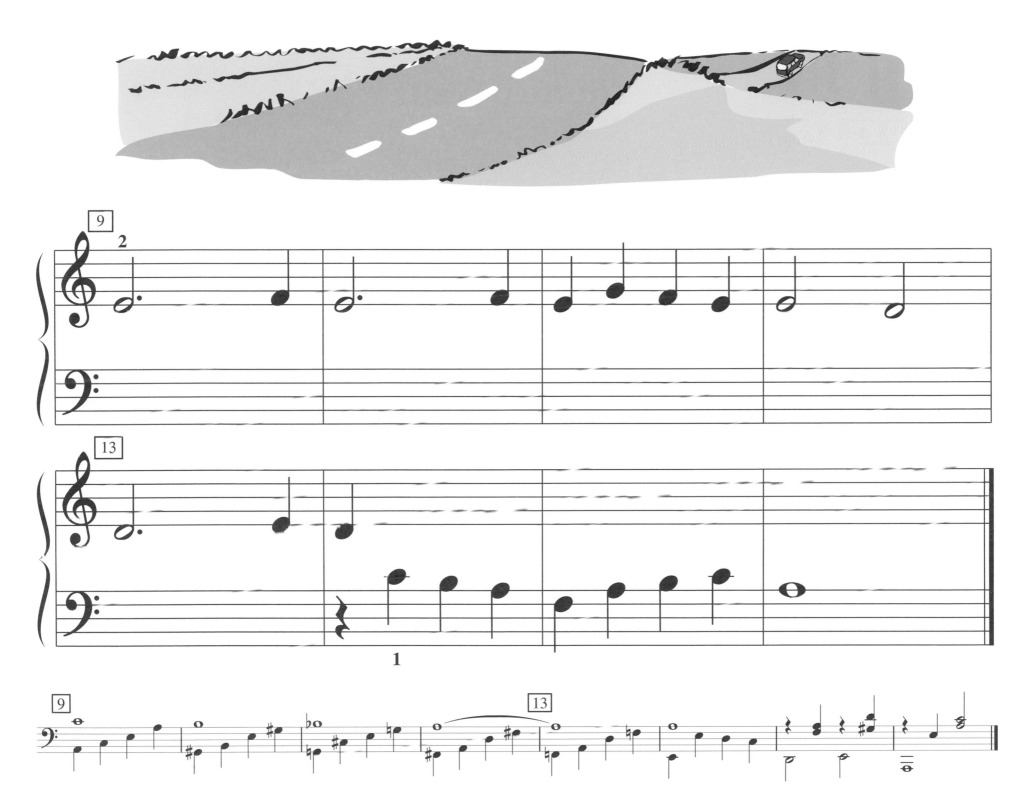

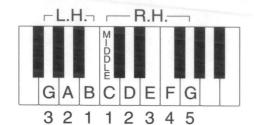

The Step Waltz

Phillip Keveren

Allegretto

mf This lit - tle waltz real - ly wrote it - self

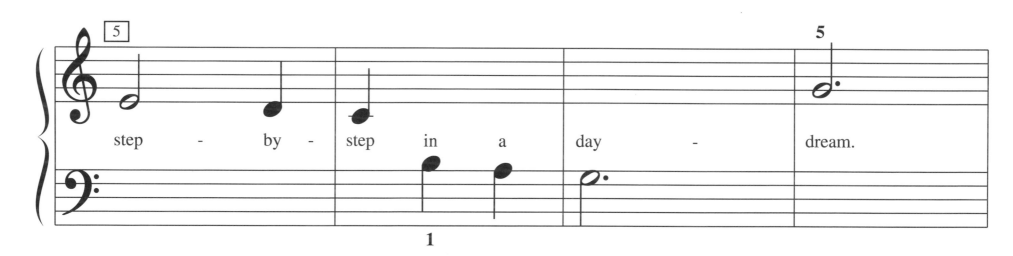

step - by - step in a day - dream.

Accompaniment (Student plays two octaves higher than written.)

Allegretto (♩ = 145)

mp

Use with Lesson Book 1, pg. 59

Note next to note it's no sym - pho - ny, but it's

per - fect for whist - ling or sing - ing.

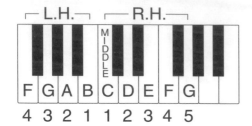

Sleepy Time

Italo Taranta

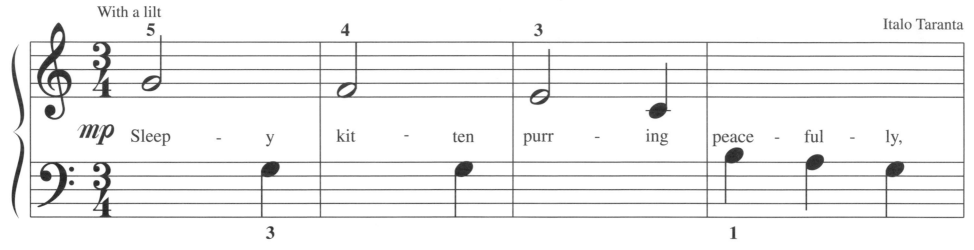

With a lilt

mp Sleep – y kit – ten purr – ing peace – ful – ly,

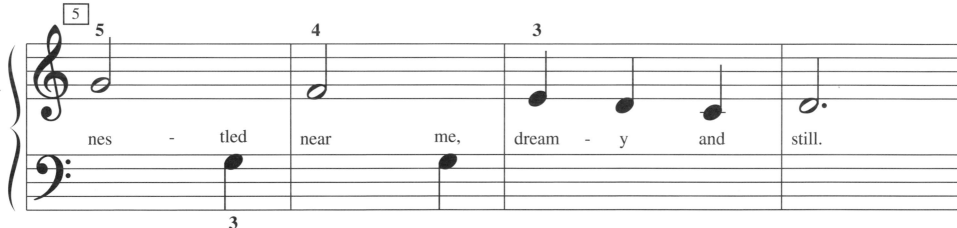

nes – tled near me, dream – y and still.

Accompaniment (Student plays two octaves higher than written.)

With a lilt (♩ = 125)

p

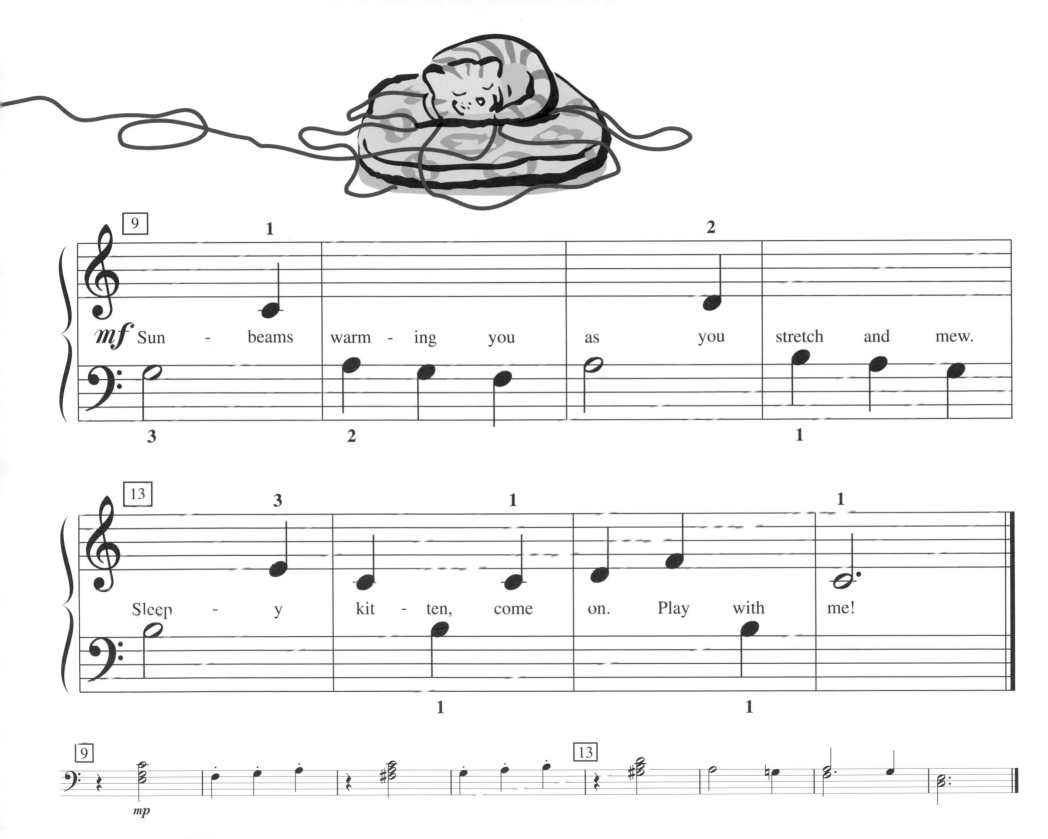

Hard As A Rock

Bill Boyd

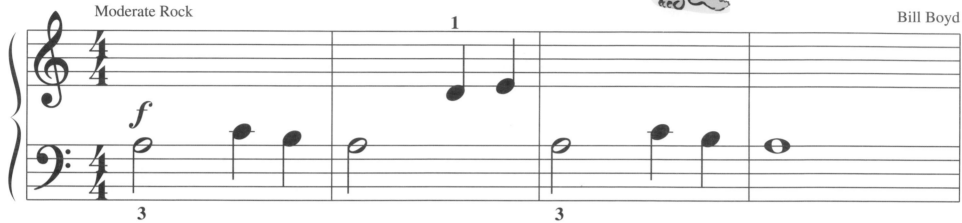

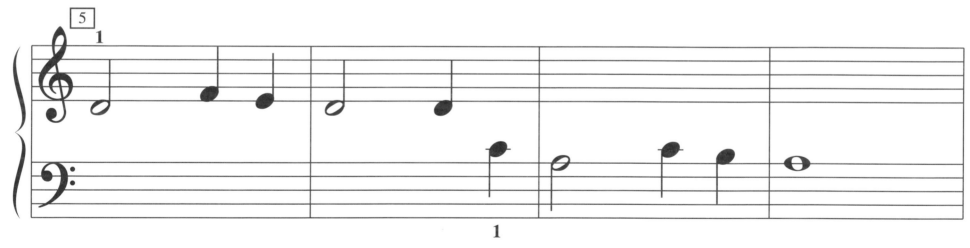

Accompaniment (Student plays one octave higher than written.)

Hal Leonard Student Piano Library

The Hal Leonard Student Piano Library has great music and solid pedagogy delivered in a truly creative and comprehensive method. It's that simple. A creative approach to learning using solid pedagogy and the best music produces skilled musicians! Great music means motivated students, inspired teachers and delighted parents. It's a method that encourages practice, progress, confidence, and best of all – success.

PIANO LESSONS BOOK 1
00296177 Book/Online Audio $10.99
00296001 Book Only $8.99

PIANO PRACTICE GAMES BOOK 1
00296002 .... $8.99

PIANO SOLOS BOOK 1
00296568 Book/Online Audio $10.99
00296003 Book Only $8.99

PIANO THEORY WORKBOOK BOOK 1
00296023 .... $7.99

PIANO TECHNIQUE BOOK 1
00296563 Book/Online Audio $9.99
00296105 Book Only $8.99

NOTESPELLER FOR PIANO BOOK 1
00296088 .... $8.99

TEACHER'S GUIDE BOOK 1
00296048 .... $8.99

PIANO LESSONS BOOK 2
00296178 Book/Online Audio $10.99
00296006 Book Only $8.99

PIANO PRACTICE GAMES BOOK 2
00296007 .... $8.99

PIANO SOLOS BOOK 2
00296569 Book/Online Audio $10.99
00296008 Book Only $8.99

PIANO THEORY WORKBOOK BOOK 2
00296024 .... $8.99

PIANO TECHNIQUE BOOK 2
00296564 Book/Online Audio $10.99
00296106 Book Only $8.99

NOTESPELLER FOR PIANO BOOK 2
00296089 .... $8.99

PIANO LESSONS BOOK 3
00296179 Book/Online Audio $10.99
00296011 Book Only $8.99

PIANO PRACTICE GAMES BOOK 3
00296012 .... $8.99

PIANO SOLOS BOOK 3
00296570 Book/Online Audio $10.99
00296013 Book Only $8.99

PIANO THEORY WORKBOOK BOOK 3
00296025 .... $8.99

PIANO TECHNIQUE BOOK 3
00296565 Book/Enhanced CD Pack $8.99
00296114 Book Only $8.99

NOTESPELLER FOR PIANO BOOK 3
00296167 .... $8.99

PIANO LESSONS BOOK 4
00296180 Book/Online Audio $10.99
00296026 Book Only $8.99

PIANO SOLOS BOOK 4
00296571 Book/Online Audio $10.99
00296028 Book Only $8.99

PIANO THEORY WORKBOOK BOOK 4
00296038 .... $8.99

PIANO TECHNIQUE BOOK 4
00296566 Book/Online Audio $10.99
00296115 Book Only $7.99

PIANO LESSONS BOOK 5
00296181 Book/Online Audio $11.99
00296041 Book Only $9.99

PIANO SOLOS BOOK 5
00296572 Book/Online Audio $12.99
00296043 Book Only $8.99

PIANO THEORY WORKBOOK BOOK 5
00296042 .... $8.99

PIANO TECHNIQUE BOOK 5
00296567 Book/Online Audio $10.99
00296116 Book Only $8.99

ALL-IN-ONE PIANO LESSONS
00296761 Book A – Book/Online Audio $12.99
00296776 Book B – Book/Online Audio $12.99
00296851 Book C – Book/Online Audio $12.99
00296852 Book D – Book/Enhanced CD Pack $12.99

Prices, contents, and availability subject to change without notice.

7777 W. BLUEMOUND RD. P.O. BOX 13819 MILWAUKEE, WI 53213

www.halleonard.com